New York

by Ellen Sturm

Consultant:
Kathleen Hulser
Public Historian
New-York Historical Society

Capstone press

Mankato, Minnesota

Capstone Press
151 Good Counsel Drive • P.O. Box 669 • Mankato, Minnesota 56002
http://www.capstone-press.com
Copyright © 2003 by Capstone Press. All rights reserved.
No part of this publication may be reproduced in whole or in part, or stored in a retrieval system, or transmitted in any form or by any means, electronic, mechanical, photocopying, recording, or otherwise, without written permission of the publisher.
For information regarding permission, write to Capstone Press,
151 Good Counsel Drive, P.O. Box 669, Dept. R, Mankato, Minnesota 56002.
Printed in the United States of America

Library of Congress Cataloging-in-Publication Data
Sturm, Ellen.
  New York/ by Ellen Sturm.
    v. cm.—(Land of Liberty)
    Includes bibliographical references and index.
    Contents: About New York—Land, climate, and wildlife—History of New York—Government and politics—Economy and resources—People and culture.
    ISBN 0-7368-1592-9 (hardcover)
  1. New York (State)—Juvenile literature. [1. New York (State)] I. Title. II. Series.
F119.3 .S77 2003
974.7—dc21   2002012470

Editorial Credits
Heather Adamson, editor; Jennifer Schonborn, series and book designer; Angi
   Gahler, illustrator; Deirdre Barton and Wanda Winch, photo researchers;
   Eric Kudalis, product planning editor

Photo Credits
Cover images: Ausable River in the Adirondack Mountains, Corbis/James
   Randklev; New York City skyline at night, Panoramic images/Jerry Driendl

Bruce Coleman Inc./Lee Rentz, 8; Bruce Coleman Inc./Diane Ali, 12–13; Bruce Coleman Inc./John Shaw, 16; Bruce Coleman Inc./Owen Tomalin, 42–43; Bruce Coleman Inc./Dan Silverstein, 46; Capstone Press/Gary Sundermeyer, 54; Corbis/Kelly-Mooney Photography, 4; Corbis/Hulton Deutsch Collection, 15; Corbis/Richard Morris Hunt, 27; Corbis/Swim Ink, 28; Corbis/Alan Scheing Photography, 32; Corbis/Gail Mooney, 38; Corbis/Michael S. Yamashita, 44; Corbis/Mitchell Gerber, 50–51; Corbis/David Muench, 63; Countdown Entertainment, 52; DigitalVision, 1; Getty Images, 41; Getty Images/Hulton Archive, 22, 36; Getty Images/Hulton Archive/Three Lions Collection, 25, 58; 911 Pictures/Michael Heller, 30; New York State Dept. of Economic Development, 29 "I ♥ NY" *is a registered trademark and service mark of the New York State Dept. of Economic Development; used with permission;* One Mile Up, Inc., 55 (both); Panoramic Images/Richard Sisk, 18–19; Paramount Press/Robert Griffing, 20; PhotoDisc, 56, 57; Unicorn Stock Photos/Jeff Greenberg, 48; U.S. Postal Service, 59

Artistic Effects
Corel, Creatas, Digital Stock, DigitalVision, PhotoDisc, Inc.

1 2 3 4 5 6 08 07 06 05 04 03

Table of Contents

Chapter 1 About New York 5

Chapter 2 Land, Climate, and Wildlife 9

Chapter 3 History of New York 21

Chapter 4 Government and Politics 33

Chapter 5 Economy and Resources 39

Chapter 6 People and Culture 47

Maps
New York Cities 7
New York's Land Features 11

Features
Recipe: Chunky Apple Molasses Muffins 54
New York's Flag and Seal 55
Almanac 56
Timeline 58
Words to Know 60
To Learn More 61
Internet Sites 61
Places to Write and Visit 62
Index 64

The Rockettes have been performing at Radio City Music Hall since 1932.

Chapter 1

About New York

The curtains open on the stage at Radio City Music Hall. The dazzling lights fall on a row of long-legged dancers. They all wear glamorous costumes and bright smiles. They move together across the stage forming a kickline. They are the Radio City Rockettes, the world's most famous precision dance troupe.

The Rockettes dance at Radio City Music Hall. This building has lush architecture and design. The marquee sign is a full city block long. With a stage reaching 60 feet (18 meters) high and 100 feet (30 meters) wide, Radio City Music Hall is the largest indoor theater in the world. Theater-goers admire the shimmering gold stage curtain. The sounds of the "Mighty Wurlitzer" organ entertain visitors. The organ's pipes fill 11 rooms.

The hall was designed to provide quality entertainment at prices ordinary people could afford during the Great Depression (1929–1939). The music hall was a sign of hope during a hard time in America. Today, Radio City Music Hall still produces top shows. More than one million people watch the Rockettes dance in the *Radio City Christmas Spectacular* each year.

The Empire State

New York is known as the Empire State. The nickname may have started back in 1784 when George Washington called the state "the seat of empire." With nearly 19 million people, New York is the third most populated state. New York's motto "Ever Upward" describes the state as well. The state works to be a leader in technology, art, trade, and culture.

New York is a large, Middle Atlantic state. It is bordered to the north by Lake Ontario and Canada. Lake Erie and Niagara Falls make up New York's western edge, while New Jersey and Pennsylvania lie to the south. Vermont, Massachusetts, and Connecticut share New York's eastern border. Long Island, part of New York, sits nearby in the Atlantic Ocean.

The Finger Lakes are in west-central New York.

Chapter 2

Land, Climate, and Wildlife

New York's landscape has plenty of water. The state has 70,000 miles (112,651 kilometers) of rivers and streams and 127 miles (204 kilometers) of Atlantic Ocean coastline. People traveled along these waterways before paved roads were built.

New York is composed of 47,214 square miles (122,284 square kilometers) of land. This area includes three major geographic regions. These regions are the Appalachian Region, the Coastal Plain, and the Central Lowland.

> **Did you know...?**
> Adirondack Park is larger than Yellowstone, Yosemite, Grand Canyon, Glacier, and Olympic National Parks combined.

Appalachian Region

The Appalachian Region covers most of New York. The region is divided into several areas.

The Appalachian Plateaus cover an area west of the Hudson Valley with rugged and hilly land. The Catskill Mountains stand in the southeastern section of the region. The Finger Lakes, long narrow lakes shaped like fingers, are also in this region. The Shawnagunk Mountains and Palisade cliffs are favorite places for rock climbers.

The Adirondack province is a 10,000-square-mile (26,000-square-kilometer) highland area in the northeast portion of the state. Mount Marcy, at 5,344 feet (1,629 meters), is the highest point in the state.

The New England Upland province meets the Coastal Plain near New York City. Hills and low mountains cover much of this area. Manhattan is located on a section of this province where strong bedrock supports the city's many skyscrapers.

New York's Land Features

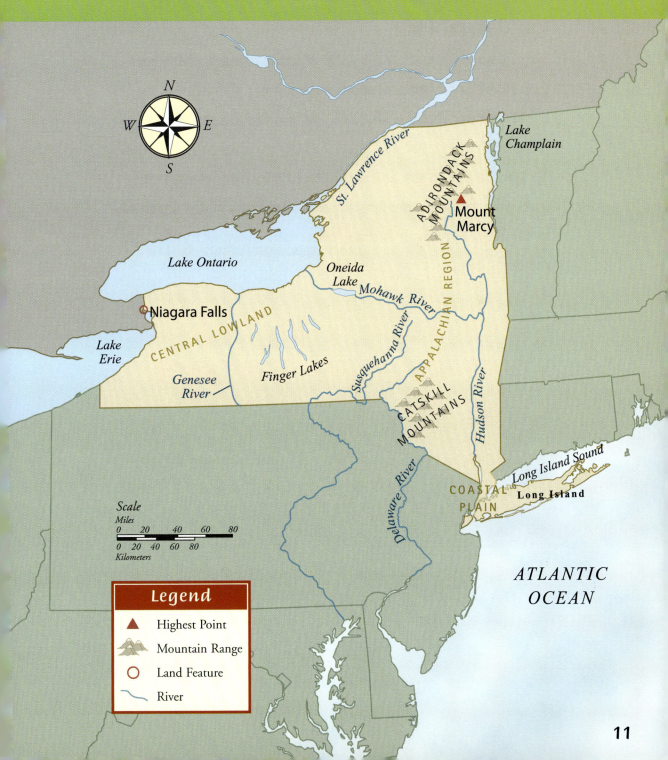

11

The Coastal Plain

The Coastal Plain stretches from Massachusetts to Mexico. Part of this plain reaches southeastern New York. Brooklyn, Staten Island, Queens, and Long Island are located on this plain.

The land is so low in the Coastal Plain that water covers parts of it and creates many bays. Oysters and clams are found in the bays. American Indians once used the oyster and clam shells for money. Long Island is known for its hundreds of

miles of beaches. The fine, white sand lining the ocean and bays makes it a popular summer recreation spot.

Central Lowland

The Central Lowland is located on the northwest border of the state along Lake Ontario and Lake Erie. The region is narrow along the shore of Lake Erie and widens as it goes north toward Buffalo. The Central Lowland is part of a larger region called the Interior Plains.

The beaches of Long Island are famous for their fine, white sand. The beaches are popular recreation spots in the summer.

The Central Lowland has many swamps and some of the country's best-known drumlin formations. Drumlins are stretched-out hills made from glaciers. These bumpy formations have the shape of upside-down egg cartons.

The state's shortest river runs through this region. The Niagara is only 35 miles (56 kilometers) long. It flows between Lake Erie and Lake Ontario and forms Niagara Falls.

Weather

New York's climate varies greatly from area to area. Along the coast, the ocean makes summers less hot and winters less cold. More snow falls near the Great Lakes.

New York normally receives about 39 inches (99 centimeters) of precipitation each year. The wettest areas are the southern slopes of the Adirondacks, the Black River Valley, the Central Catskills, and Long Island. The driest areas are along Lake Champlain, the St. Lawrence River, and Lake Ontario. Syracuse, Rochester, and Buffalo receive large amounts of snow.

Niagara Falls

Every minute at Niagara Falls, millions of gallons of rushing water cascade over a 180-foot (55 meter) drop. The water creates a thunderous roar. Made up of three falls, this natural wonder crosses the border between New York and Canada.

Many people have performed stunts at the falls. French tightrope walker "Blondin," pictured, crossed Niagara Falls on a highwire many times in the 1800s. Each time, he did it while doing a different trick. Once he was blindfolded, and another time he pushed a wheelbarrow. One time, he even stopped halfway across to cook an omelet.

In 1901, Annie Edison Taylor, a 63-year-old schoolteacher, was the first person to survive going over the falls in a barrel. Today, such stunts are illegal.

Trees and Flowers

Forests once covered most of New York. Loggers cut down many trees and shipped them on the Hudson River. Now only about half of the land is covered with trees. About 150 types of trees grow in New York, including pine, beech, yellow birch, hickory, and oak. The state tree is the sugar maple. People collect the tree's sweet sap to make syrup.

The sugar maple is New York's state tree. The sugar maple's leaves turn bright orange, yellow, or red in fall.

Many types of flowers grow in New York. Buttercups, violets, and wild roses grow along the borders of forests. The rose became the state flower in 1955. In wetter areas, cattails, impatiens, and marsh marigolds are common.

Wildlife

In summer, birds such as robins, mourning doves, and wrens live in most areas of New York. Many birds migrate through New York on their way south for the winter. The peregrine falcon has found a permanent home among the skyscrapers and high bridges of New York City.

Common New York mammals include bobcats, coyotes, raccoons, foxes, and striped gray squirrels. Moose are so common in the north that moose crossing signs line the roads to warn drivers. The beaver is the state animal.

A variety of reptiles and amphibians also make the state their home. Frogs, salamanders, lizards, freshwater turtles, sea turtles, and snakes are found in New York.

More than 165 fish species inhabit the state's waters. Common freshwater fish include bass, perch, pike, salmon, and sunfish. The brook trout is the state fish. Bluefish, clams, flounder, oysters, and swordfish live in bays and ocean waters.

The ocean waters near New York City and Long Island are home to whales, dolphins, and seals.

Environmental Challenges

New York has a long history of protecting its land. New York was the first state to declare land "forever wild" by creating the Adirondack and Catskill forest preserves. In 1885, it became the first state to establish a state park, the Niagara Reservation.

New York also works to protect animals that are in danger of extinction. The river otter, karner blue butterfly, and bog turtle are a few of the animals protected by the state.

New York struggles with pollution. The many homes and businesses in the state create water and air pollution. New York City produces much more garbage than it can process or store. The state is trying to control pollution and excess garbage with disposal permits and government programs.

Niagara Falls is part of the nation's first state park. Niagara Falls is actually three waterfalls between New York and Canada.

Seneca Indians, part of the Iroquois Confederacy, lived and traveled throughout central New York.

Chapter 3

History of New York

The Algonquian and Iroquois Indians were living in New York by A.D. 1000. The Algonquian group includes the Mahican, Delaware, Wappinger, Montauk, and Munsee. During this time, they lived in the southeast section of the state and along the Hudson River and Lake Champlain. They were farmers who also fished, hunted, and gathered food.

At the same time, the Iroquois lived in central New York and the Great Lakes area. They also were farmers. Families lived together in large bark-covered homes called longhouses. The Mohawk, Oneida, Onondaga, Cayuga, and Seneca formed the Iroquois Confederacy, or Five Nations, around 1570. The U.S. Constitution uses some of their ideas.

European Explorers and Settlers

European explorers came to New York more than 400 years ago. Samuel de Champlain and a group of French fur traders explored northern New York in 1603. Henry Hudson worked for the Dutch and explored the river now called the Hudson in 1609. He claimed the region for the Netherlands.

New York gets its name from James, the Duke of York. The land was given to the duke by his brother, King Charles II of England, in 1664.

The Dutch permanently settled in New York in 1624. They formed a colony in the Hudson Valley and called it New Netherlands. On Manhattan Island, the Dutch established New Amsterdam in 1617. New York City stands on the island today.

> **Did you know...?**
> Legend says that the New Amsterdam colony's governor, Peter Minuit, bought the island of Manhattan from American Indians for $24. The Indians may have believed they were renting the island to the colonists for hunting.

In 1664, King Charles II of England took over the region. He claimed that England's John Cabot found the region while exploring in 1497. Charles gave the land to his brother James, the Duke of York. The southern part of the state was then named New York in honor of James.

The beaver population and river trade made the French interested in New York. In 1669, French explorer René-Robert Cavelier, known as Sieur de La Salle, explored the Niagara region and built a fort at Lake Champlain. From 1754 to 1763, France and Great Britain fought in the French and Indian War. American Indians helped both sides. Great Britain won in 1763. The British forced France to give up a large area of land that included parts of New York.

Revolutionary War

In the 1770s, about half of New York's people stayed loyal to Great Britain. Others protested Britain's high taxes. Many African American slaves sided with the British who promised to free them. Five days after the 13 colonies declared independence, the people of New York met to make their own government. New York formed as a state on April 20, 1777.

New Yorkers supplied food, clothing, lead, and iron to General George Washington and the Continental Army. Almost a third of the battles in the Revolutionary War (1775–1783) were fought in New York. Fort Ticonderoga was the site of the colonists' first victory. The Battle of Saratoga stopped the British from taking over the Hudson River.

A New Beginning

After winning the war, colonists needed to form their own government. New Yorkers Alexander Hamilton and John Jay helped convince the nation to adopt the Constitution. On July 26, 1788, New York became the 11th state of the new country.

New York City was chosen to be the nation's first capital. The city held a celebration when George Washington became

The British were forced to surrender in the Battle of Saratoga. This surrender was a turning point in the Revolutionary War.

president on April 30, 1789. New York City remained the nation's capital until 1790.

State of Immigrants

By 1860, New York City was the largest U.S. city. One million people lived there. Half of the people had been born

25

"Give me your tired, your poor, your huddled masses yearning to breathe free."
—from "The New Colossus" by New York poet Emma Lazarus, 1883

in other countries. Most immigrants came to America through New York City and many stayed there to live. The potato famine in Ireland forced many Irish to come to America to find jobs. Many worked on the Erie Canal.

On July 4, 1884, France gave the Statue of Liberty to the United States as a symbol of America's mission. America wanted to help people from all over the world get a better life. President Grover Cleveland dedicated the Statue of Liberty in New York Harbor on October 28, 1886.

In 1892, Ellis Island opened in New York Harbor. It became the main entrance for immigrants. About 12 million immigrants arrived at Ellis Island. Many Jewish, Irish, and German immigrants entered the United States through Ellis Island.

New York City was a mix of culture from all over the world. People called it a melting pot of people. Even today, many different languages are spoken in New York City.

Role in Wars

New York supported the United States in many wars. Much of the War of 1812 (1812–1814) was fought along New York's border with Canada. Captain Thomas Macdonough defeated

The Statue of Liberty was a gift from France. The statue was shipped in 350 pieces. It was put together and set in place in 1886. The statue's right arm is 42 feet (13 meters) long.

Uncle Sam

People often refer to the government as "Uncle Sam." This term is believed to have started during the War of 1812. A New York meatpacker named Sam Wilson marked his barrels of meat with the letters "U.S." People joked that the meat came from Uncle Sam.

Uncle Sam eventually became a symbol for the government. New Yorker Montgomery Flagg painted the most famous image of Uncle Sam in 1916. The army used Flagg's Uncle Sam image on posters to encourage support for World War I.

the British on Lake Champlain in the Battle of Plattsburgh. He prevented the British from entering New York.

New York sided with the North in the Civil War (1861–1865). The North and South fought over state's rights and the issue of slavery. New York provided more soldiers, supplies, and money to the North than any other state.

New York also played a role in other U.S. wars. More than 500,000 New York men were drafted and 14,000 were killed in World War I (1914–1918). New York's factories made airplanes, ships, and guns for both world wars. New York also produced supplies for the Korean War (1950–1953) and the Vietnam War (1954–1975).

Difficult Times

In the 1970s, New York experienced a sharp fall in its economy. Companies moved to states where it was cheaper to operate. People followed the jobs and left the state. New York worked hard to bring businesses back. The state lowered taxes and promoted its natural resources. It also started an "I Love New

The "I Love New York" campaign celebrated its 25th year in 2002. The famous heart logo has appeared on T-shirts, billboards, and key chains.

Firefighters and rescue workers stand in the ruins of the World Trade Center Towers. It took more than three months to put out the fire and nearly one year to remove all the debris.

York" ad campaign. By 1990, the state's population was growing again with 18 million people living there.

On September 11, 2001, New York City was the site of an attack on America. Terrorists hijacked four airplanes and flew two of them into the 110-story Twin Towers of the World Trade Center in Manhattan. Firefighters, police, and rescue workers rushed into the buildings to help. The towers collapsed and more than 2,700 people were killed. On the same day, terrorists also flew a plane into the Pentagon in Washington, D.C. Another plane crashed in Pennsylvania.

People all over the world wanted to help New York City. Volunteer rescue and cleanup crews arrived. Some people sent food and clothes. Others gave money or blood. Hundreds of dog boots were donated so rescue dogs could walk safely through the rubble.

It took more than three months to put out the fire from the crashed planes and fallen buildings. Crews worked day and night to remove 1.8 million tons (1.6 million metric tons) of rubble and steel. More than 30,000 New Yorkers lost their jobs after the attacks. The state is again trying to help families and businesses stay in New York.

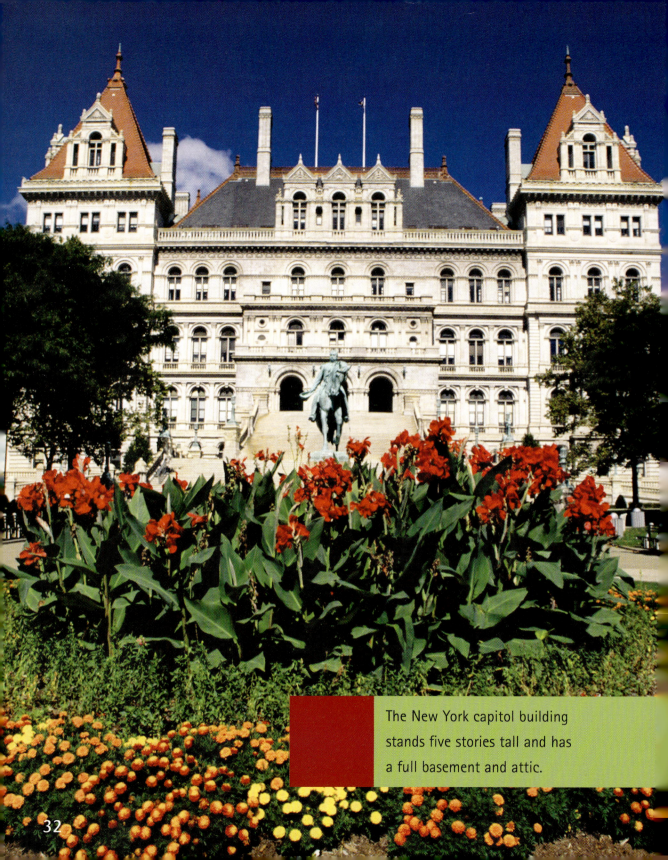

The New York capitol building stands five stories tall and has a full basement and attic.

32

Chapter 4

Government and Politics

The first government of New York grew out of the Revolutionary War. A Council of Safety governed New York until the State Convention finalized the state constitution in 1777. On July 30, 1777, George Clinton became the state's first governor.

The legislature met in Kingston and other cities throughout the state until 1796. In 1797, the legislature began meeting in Albany. The city has been the state's capital since then.

Today, New York's biggest conflicts rise between New York City and the rest of the state. The millions of people living in the city have different problems than the less densely populated areas.

State Government

New York's state government has three branches. They are the executive, legislative, and judicial branches.

The governor of New York heads the executive branch. He or she names officials, prepares the state's budget, and enforces state laws.

The legislature is composed of the Senate and the Assembly. The branches have equal power. They make laws. The Senate has 61 members. The Assembly has 150 members who represent 150 districts.

The judicial branch includes the courts and judges in New York. Legal trials take place at many levels from county courts to the Court of Appeals, New York's highest court. Voters elect supreme court judges to 14-year terms.

New York is fairly evenly divided between Republicans and Democrats. In most of the state, there are slightly more Republicans. But in New York City, Democrats outnumber Republicans five to one. Republicans have generally controlled the state Senate, and Democrats have controlled the Assembly.

New York's State Government

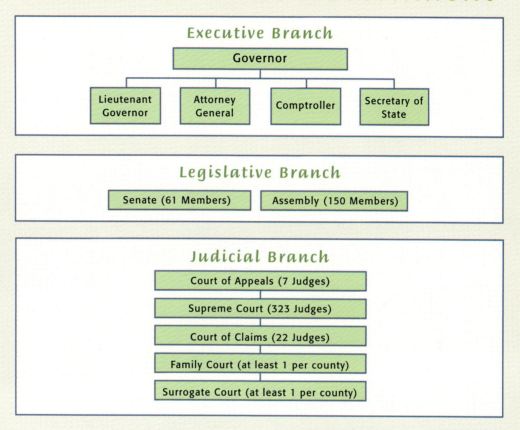

Local Government

There are 62 counties in New York. Town boards and city supervisors or elected officials oversee 57 of them. New York City's five counties are called boroughs. They have a special form of government because of the city's large population and area. Manhattan, Brooklyn, Queens, Staten Island, and the Bronx make up New York City boroughs.

A Famous Duel

Alexander Hamilton and Aaron Burr were political enemies in New York. Hamilton was a Federalist. Burr was a member of the Republican Party.

When Burr decided to run for governor of New York, Hamilton spoke out against him. Burr thought Hamilton said things that were mean and untrue. Burr challenged Hamilton to a pistol duel. Hamilton agreed.

The duel took place July 11, 1804. It was held in New Jersey because duels were illegal in New York. At the signal, Hamilton fired into the air as Burr shot him in the spine. Hamilton died the next day.

New York in National Government

New York elects two U.S. senators and 31 members of the House of Representatives. Because New York has 33 electoral votes, it is an important state in presidential elections. Since 1880, New Yorkers have voted for the winning presidential candidate in all but five elections.

Famous Governors

Many New York governors have moved to national politics. They have become presidents, vice presidents, or supreme court justices.

Theodore Roosevelt became New York's governor in 1899. He served as President William McKinley's vice president and later became president. Roosevelt won the Nobel Peace Prize in 1906.

Franklin D. Roosevelt, New York's 44th governor, was elected in 1928. He governed one year before the stock market crashed and the Great Depression (1929–1939) began. He started "New Deal" programs in New York to create jobs and help end the Depression. Roosevelt spread the programs across the country after he became president in 1933. He was the only president to be elected to four terms.

Nelson A. Rockefeller was elected governor of New York four times. President Gerald Ford chose Rockefeller to be his vice president in August 1974.

Department stores, banks, and other businesses have headquarters in New York City.

Chapter 5

Economy and Resources

New York's natural resources help make it a leader in industry and agriculture. The state has plenty of water for homes, factories, and farms. The state's waters are also used to transport goods. The glaciers that covered New York made some of the soil good for farming. The glaciers also left behind stone, zinc, salt, and other materials now mined in the state.

Many of the state's industrial workers live in the New York City area. The city generates much of the state's industrial income. It is also the world's leading financial center. Much of the nation's trade is carried on in New York City's offices.

"Wall Street is motivated primarily by emotions—fear and greed."
—Wall Street saying

New York's other cities are also important to the state's economy. Buffalo is the state's second largest city and an important industrial center in western New York. Companies in Rochester make camera equipment, hospital supplies, and scientific instruments. The city of Yonkers manufactures plastics and chemicals. Syracuse is a distribution center for electrical and transportation equipment. Albany hosts most of the state government offices.

Service Industries

Service industries make up the largest part of New York's money-making industries. Banking, insurance, and real estate contribute the most. The New York Stock Exchange, founded in 1792, has become the center of world finance.

Manufacturing

Manufactured goods produced in New York have a value of about $90 billion each year. New York has more than 25,000 factories. Over one million New Yorkers work in factories.

Wall Street

Wall Street is a small street in New York City. Wall Street got its name from a wall that protected Dutch colonists from Indian raids and other colonies' armies. Today, Wall Street is a symbol of world finance and banking. The New York Stock Exchange now sits in the Wall Street district. More than 3,000 companies have their stocks listed there.

At the sound of the opening bell each day, frantic stock trading begins. Traders use phones, pagers, and monitors to receive customer requests for trading. The traders shout and use hand signals to find others who want to swap. They work fast because they want to make as many trades as possible before the closing bell rings.

About 10 percent of the nation's printing and publishing is done in New York. Random House and Penguin Putnam are book publishers with offices in New York. More than 2,000 different magazines and newspapers are produced in New York.

New York is also a center of instrument manufacturing. The state makes navigation equipment, surgery and medical instruments, and tools to measure electricity. Schenectady is the home of General Electric, a company that makes electric equipment.

Agriculture

Farmland makes up 7.7 million acres (3.1 million hectares), or about one-fourth, of New York's land area. About 38,000 farms cover New York.

Livestock and livestock products provide most of New York's agricultural income. New York ranks third in milk production. Hogs and sheep are raised for meat.

Many poultry farms are located in Suffolk County on Long Island and in Sullivan County in the Catskills. Suffolk County is famous for its ducks. It provides more than half of the ducks in the United States. New York is a leader in egg production.

Crops provide about one-third of New York's agricultural income. Hay and corn are the state's leading field crops. They are used mainly as feed for dairy cattle. Other important

Grapes grow in vineyards throughout the state.

crops are beans, potatoes, cabbage, onions, oats, wheat, and small vegetables.

Fruit is another important agricultural product. New York is second behind Washington in producing apples. The state is third in grapes, behind California and Washington. Other important fruit crops include strawberries, tart cherries, pears, and plums.

Fishing is a large industry in New York. Many fresh fish markets can be found in Long Island.

Natural Resources

The state's many trees are a valuable resource. New York competes with Vermont for the top spot in maple syrup production. Forestry supplies trees for the state's wood pulp and paper industry. Hardwoods are used for building furniture.

New York's bodies of water provide a healthy fishing industry. Long Island Sound is known for its oysters and clams. Flounder, lobster, scallops, and striped bass can also be found there.

Some mining takes place in the state. Crushed stone, salt, sand, and gravel are used for construction. Wine-red garnet is mined in the southeastern Adirondacks. Garnet is used for watch jewels and in sandpaper. It is the state gem. Zinc and iron are two metals mined in New York.

Did you know...?
New York is the largest grape juice producer in the United States. New York's Chautauqua County is the second largest grape growing region in the country.

More than 40 percent of the state's population lives in New York City.

Chapter 6

People and Culture

People from many ethnic backgrounds and religions live in New York. Italians, Irish, Germans, and Eastern Europeans all live in the state. More than three million African Americans live in New York. This number is more than in any other state. More than one million Puerto Ricans live in New York City. Many Latin Americans, Chinese, South Asians, and Arab Americans also make New York their home.

The largest religious group in New York is Roman Catholic. More than half of the state's population follow other religions. Baptists and Methodists make up the largest Protestant groups. New York also has a large Jewish community. More than one-fourth of the Jews in the United States live in New York.

Transportation

Cars, trains, boats, and subways all help manage the state's travelers. Traffic jams on the roads leading to New York City bridges and tunnels are common. Many people live outside the city and drive into the city to work. Many others take trains. Railroad commuters come into New York City at Grand Central Station or Pennsylvania Station. Within Manhattan, subways run underground. Ferry boats run from Staten Island and New Jersey into Manhattan.

Traffic jams are common in New York City. Many people take subways or trains to avoid the city's traffic problems.

New York's Ethnic Background

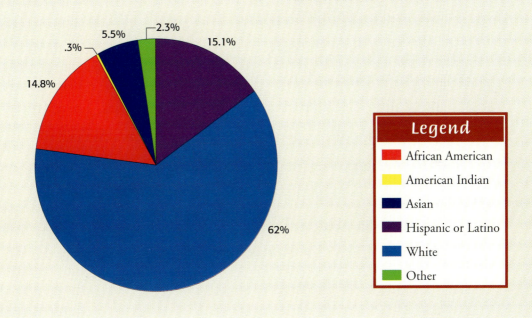

Recreation and Entertainment

Millions of tourists visit New York. More than 17 million people visit New York City each year. New York offers a variety of arts and recreation activities for its citizens and visitors to enjoy.

New York's natural features can be experienced in 151 state parks. At Letchworth State Park, the Genesee River passes through a huge gorge that is 600 feet (183 meters) deep. It is often called "The Grand Canyon of the East." Plenty of hiking trails are found in Adirondack Park. The park measures

6 million acres (2 million hectares). Downhill ski areas are located throughout the state. For summertime fun, New York has many lakeside and ocean beaches.

New York City offers plenty of cultural activities. There are 1,300 museums and galleries, 64 performing arts centers, and 230 theaters. The Guggenheim Museum's architecture was designed by Frank Lloyd Wright. It holds work from artists like Edgar Degas, Pablo Picasso, Camille Pissarro, and Vincent van Gogh. Some of the world's best actors star on the 38 theaters of Broadway.

Professional Sports

New York has many pro sports teams. The New York Yankees play baseball in Yankee Stadium in the Bronx. The New York Mets play in Shea Stadium in Queens. Pro football teams include the Jets and the Giants, who both play at the Meadowlands in New Jersey. The Buffalo Bills are another popular football team. The New York Knicks are the state's pro basketball team. Three hockey teams, the New York Rangers, New York Islanders, and Buffalo Sabres, have home ice in New York.

Broadway shows use detailed sets and colorful costumes. Many of the world's best actors and musicians perform in theaters on Broadway.

New Year's Eve in Times Square

Since 1907, New Yorkers have welcomed the new year by lowering a ball in Times Square in New York City. The ball has dropped at midnight every year except 1942 and 1943 when wartime dimouts prevented it.

The first ball was made of iron and wood. It was decorated with 100 lightbulbs. Today, the ball is covered by 500 crystal triangles and has almost 700 lightbulbs.

More than 500,000 people gather in Times Square each year to watch the ball. Millions more watch TV to see it drop. The celebration usually includes music, fireworks, and confetti.

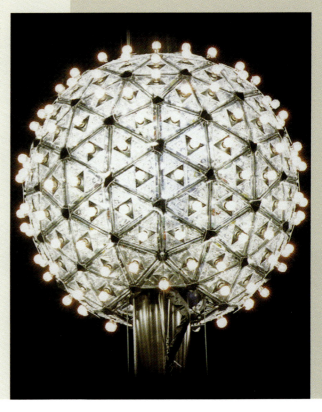

New York also hosts many special sports events. In 2002, the U.S. Open Golf Championship was held at Bethpage on Long Island. The U.S. Open for tennis is held at Arthur Ashe

> *"Buildings are important, but the spirit of New York is its people, free people dedicated to democracy . . . ."*
> —Rudy Giuliani, 107th mayor of New York

Stadium in Queens. Belmont Park is a famous horse racetrack located on Long Island. The Belmont Stakes takes place there.

Perceptions

New Yorkers are sometimes thought of as rude, busy, cityfolk who do not care about other people. That image mostly comes from TV shows or movies that show crowds of people walking the streets of New York City and ignoring each other. But New York City is actually an amazing display of people getting along. It is a center for fashion, entertainment, art, business, and world culture. Not many cities have that kind of balance.

The state of New York is more than city life. The media often does not show the mountains, fields, or orchards that also make up the state. New Yorkers are not all the same. Still most are hard working, creative people who welcome different ideas. This quality gives New York a personality unlike any other state.

Recipe: Chunky Apple Molasses Muffins

The apple muffin became New York's state muffin in 1987. New York ranks second in the country in growing apples.

Ingredients

2 cups (480 mL) flour
¼ cup (60 mL) sugar
1 tablespoon (15 mL) baking powder
1 teaspoon (5 mL) ground cinnamon
¼ teaspoon (1.2 mL) salt
1 apple peeled, cored, and chopped
½ cup (120 mL) milk
¼ cup (60 mL) molasses
¼ cup (60 mL) vegetable oil
1 large egg

Equipment

paper muffin liners
muffin pan
large bowl
dry-ingredient measuring cups
measuring spoons
large spoon
small bowl
liquid measuring cup
electric mixer
pot holders

What You Do

1. Heat oven to 450°F (240°C). Put paper liners in cups of muffin pan. Set pan aside.

2. In a large bowl, stir flour, sugar, baking powder, cinnamon, salt, and apples. Set aside.

3. In a small bowl, use electric mixer to beat together milk, molasses, oil, and egg. Pour the mixture into the large bowl. Stir with a spoon until the two are blended.

4. Fill the lined muffin cups with the blended batter. Put in oven and bake for 5 minutes.

5. Turn oven down to 350°F (180°C) and bake for 15 minutes. Use pot holders to take muffins out of oven. Let them cool for 5 minutes. Remove muffins from pan to finish cooling.

Makes 12 muffins

New York's Flag and Seal

New York's Flag

The New York flag was adopted in 1778. The flag is dark blue with the State Coat of Arms in the center.

New York's State Seal

The Great Seal of New York was established in 1777. In 1778, it was changed slightly to include the complete State Coat of Arms. The Coat of Arms shows Liberty and Justice standing beside a shield. Liberty holds a Phrygian cap on a stick. In old times, these caps were given to freed slaves. At Liberty's feet is a crown to show the state's freedom from Britain. Justice holds a sword and a scale. These symbols represent the fairness needed in government. The shield has a picture of the sun rising behind a range of mountains. In front of the mountains, boats cross the Hudson River to show trade. Above the shield is an American bald eagle. Below the shield a banner reads, "Excelsior," which means "ever upward."

Almanac

General Facts

Nickname: Empire State

Population: 18,976,457 (U.S. Census 2000)
Population rank: 3rd

Capital: Albany

Largest cities: New York, Buffalo, Rochester, Yonkers, Syracuse

Geography

Area: 54,475 square miles (141,090 square kilometers)
Size Rank: 27th

Highest Point: Mount Marcy, 5,344 feet (1629 meters)

Lowest Point: Atlantic coastline, sea level

Agriculture

Agricultural products: dairy products, cattle, vegetables, apples, grapes

Climate

Average winter temperature: 23 degrees Fahrenheit (minus 5 degrees Celsius)

Average summer temperature: 67 degrees Fahrenheit (19 degrees Celsius)

Annual precipitation: 39 inches (99 centimeters)

Apple

Bay scallop

Symbols

Animal: Beaver

Bird: Bluebird

Fish: Brook Trout

Flower: Rose

Fruit: Apple

Gem: Garnet

Economy

Natural resources: Water, trees, stone, zinc, iron, garnets

Types of industry: Finance, printing and publishing, scientific instruments, photographic equipment, tourism, fishing

Symbols

Muffin: Apple

Shell: Bay scallop

Song: "I Love New York," by Steve Karmen

Tree: Sugar maple

Government

First governor: George Clinton

Statehood: July 26, 1788 (11th state)

U.S. Representatives: 31

U.S. Senators: 2

U.S. electoral votes: 33

Counties: 62

57

Timeline

State History

1609
Henry Hudson explores the region for the Dutch.

1624
New Netherlands colony is founded.

1664
The British conquer the area and rename it New York.

1788
On July 26, New York becomes the 11th state.

1825
Erie canal opens.

U.S. History

1570
Iroquois Confederacy forms.

1620
Pilgrims start the Plymouth colony.

1775–1783
The American Colonies fight for independence from Great Britain during the Revolutionary War.

1812–1814
The U.S. fights Great Britain in the War of 1812.

1861–1865
The North and South fight against each other in the Civil War.

1886
President Grover Cleveland dedicates the Statue of Liberty.

1929
Governor Franklin Delano Roosevelt starts New Deal programs to help New Yorkers.

1970
Companies leave New York and many people lose their jobs.

2001
On September 11, terrorists fly two airplanes into the World Trade Center in New York City.

1914–1918
World War I is fought; the U.S. enters the war in 1917.

1929–1939
The Great Depression causes financial struggles.

1939–1945
World War II is fought; the U.S. enters the war in 1941.

1964
Congress passes the Civil Rights Act, which makes discrimination illegal.

Words to Know

bedrock (BED-rok)—the solid layer of rock under the soil

duel (DOO-uhl)—a formal fight between two people with guns or swords; duels have strict rules.

ethnic (ETH-nik)—of a group of people who share the same national origins, language, or culture

garnet (GAR-nit)—a dark red stone

glacier (GLAY-shur)—a slow-moving sheet of ice found in mountains and polar regions

gorge (GORJ)—a deep, narrow valley with steep sides

immigrant (IM-uh-gruhnt)—a person who comes to another country to live permanently

marquee (mar-KEE)—a large sign outside of a theater entrance listing shows and events

migrate (MYE-grate)—to move from one place to another when seasons change or when food is scarce

troupe (TROOP)—a group of stage performers

To Learn More

Capstone Press Geography Department. *New York.* One Nation. Mankato, Minn.: Capstone Press, 2003.

Englar, Mary. *The Iroquois: The Six Nations Confederacy.* American Indian Nations. Mankato, Minn.: Bridgestone Books, 2003.

Krizner, L.J. *Peter Stuyvesant: New Amsterdam and the Origins of New York.* The Library of American Lives and Times. New York: PowerPlus Books, 2001.

Louis, Nancy. *Ground Zero.* War on Terrorism. Edina, Minn.: ABDO, 2002.

Internet Sites

Track down many sites about New York.
Visit the FACT HOUND at *http://www.facthound.com*

IT IS EASY! IT IS FUN!
1) Go to *http://www.facthound.com*
2) Type in: 0736815929
3) Click on "FETCH IT" and FACT HOUND will find several links hand-picked by our editors.

Relax and let our pal FACT HOUND do the research for you!

Places to Write and Visit

National Baseball Hall of Fame and Museum
25 Main Street
P.O. Box 590
Cooperstown, NY 13326

New York State Department of Commerce
Division of Tourism
1 Commerce Plaza
Albany, NY 12245

New-York Historical Society
2 West 77th Street
New York, NY 10024

NYS Department of State
41 State Street
Albany, New York 12231-0001

Statue of Liberty National Monument
Liberty Island
New York, NY 10004

Snow covers White Face Mountain in Adirondack Park.

Index

Adirondacks, 14, 18, 45, 63
agriculture, 39, 42–44
American Indians, 20, 23, 41
    Algonquian, 21
    Iroquois, 21
animals. See wildlife
Appalachian Region, 9, 10
Atlantic Ocean, 6, 9

Broadway, 50, 51
Burr, Aaron, 36

Canada, 6, 15, 27
Catskills, 10, 14, 18, 43
Central Lowland, 9, 13–14
Charles II, King, 22, 23
climate, 14
Clinton, George, 33
Coastal Plain, 9, 10, 12–13

drumlin, 14
Duke of York, 22, 23

economy, 29, 39–45
Ellis Island, 26
Erie Canal, 26

Finger Lakes, 8, 10
flag, 55
flowers, 17
Fort Ticonderoga, 24

government, 19, 24, 33–37
Great Depression, 6, 37

Hamilton, Alexander, 24, 36

immigrants, 25–26
Iroquois Confederacy, 20, 22

Jay, John, 24

Lake Champlain, 14, 21, 23
Lake Erie, 6, 13, 14
Lake Ontario, 6, 13, 14
La Salle, René-Robert Cavelier de, 23
Long Island, 6, 12–13, 14, 18, 43, 52, 53
Long Island Sound, 45

manufacturing, 40–41
Mount Marcy, 10

natural resources, 29, 39, 45
New York City, 10, 17, 18, 19, 23, 24–25, 26, 31, 33, 35, 38, 39, 41, 46, 47, 48, 49, 53
Niagara Falls, 14, 15, 19

population, 6, 31, 35, 46, 47
publishing, 41

Radio City Music Hall, 4, 5–6
rivers, 9
    Genesee River, 49
    Hudson River, 16, 21, 22, 24, 55
    Niagara River, 14
    St. Lawrence River, 14

Rockefeller, Nelson A., 37
Rockettes, 4, 5–6
Roosevelt, Franklin D., 37
Roosevelt, Theodore, 37

Saratoga, Battle of, 24, 25
sports, 51–53
state seal, 55
Statue of Liberty, 26, 27

Times Square, 52
tourism, 49–50
trees, 16

Uncle Sam, 28

Wall Street, 40, 41
Washington, George, 6, 24–25
wildlife, 17–18, 19
World Trade Center, 30, 31
World War I, 28